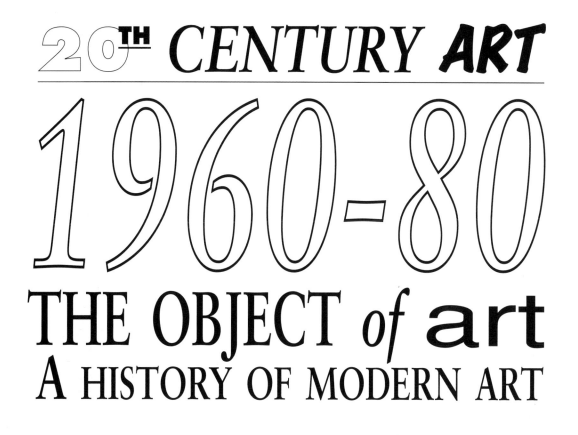

20TH CENTURY ART

1960-80

THE OBJECT of art

A HISTORY OF MODERN ART

20TH CENTURY ART – 1960-80
was produced by

David West 🏃🏃 Children's Books
7 Princeton Court
55 Felsham Road
London SW15 1AZ

Picture Research: Brooks Krikler Research
Picture Editor: Carlotta Cooper

First published in Great Britain in 2000 by
Heinemann Library, Halley Court, Jordan Hill,
Oxford OX2 8EJ, a division of Reed Educational and
Professional Publishing Limited.

OXFORD MELBOURNE AUCKLAND
JOHANNESBURG BLANTYRE GABORONE
IBADAN PORTSMOUTH (NH) USA CHICAGO

Copyright © 2000 David West Children's Books

For Adam

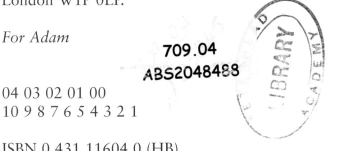

04 03 02 01 00
10 9 8 7 6 5 4 3 2 1

ISBN 0 431 11604 0 (HB)
ISBN 0 431 11611 3 (PB)

British Library Cataloguing in Publication Data

Oliver, Clare
1960-1980 the object of art. - (Twentieth century
art)
1. Art, Modern - 20th century - Juvenile literature
I. Title
709'.046

Printed and bound in Italy

PHOTO CREDITS :
Abbreviations: t-top, m-middle, b-bottom, r-right,
l-left, c-centre.

Cover & page 12-13 - Bradford Art
Galleries/Bridgeman Art Library. Page 3 & 21 -
Corbis/Page. 4t, 5b, 6b, 8t, 9b, 10l, 11m & b, 12t,
13br, 16t, 18b, 19t, 20 both, 21b, 23 both, 24t, 26r,
27 all & 28 both. 4b & 8b - Hulton Getty Collection.
5 & 13t - AKG London©Apple Records. 6t & 9t -
Bridgeman Art Library©ADAGP, Paris & DACS,
London 2000. 7 & 15t - AKG London. 10r - Courtesy
XXO Mobilier et Design, Paris. 11t - Bridgeman Art
Library©The Andy Warhol Foundation for the Visual
Arts Inc./ARS, NY & DACS London 2000. 12bl -
Caroline Graville/Redferns. 15b - Bridgeman Art
Library©ARS, NY & DACS London 2000. 16b -
Christies Images©DACS 2000. 17b -
Corbis©succession Marcel Duchamp/ADAGP, Paris &
DACS, London 2000. 18t, 25 & 29r - Bridgeman Art
Library. 19b - Reproduced by kind permission of
Gilbert & George, with thanks to the Anthony
d'Offay Gallery. 22 - Tate Gallery©Carl Andre/VAGA,
New York/DACS, London 2000. 24b - Private
collection/Bridgeman Art Library. 26l - Corbally
Stourton Contemporary Art/Bridgeman Art Library.
29l - AKG London/Private collection.

*The publishers have made every effort to contact all
the relevant copyright holders and apologise for any
inadvertent omissions.*

*The dates in brackets after a person's
name give the years that he or she lived.
The date that follows a painting's title and the
artist's name, gives the year it was painted.
'C.' stands for circa, meaning about or
approximately.*

*An explanation of difficult words can be
found in the glossary on page 30.*

20TH CENTURY ART

1960-80

THE OBJECT of art

A HISTORY OF MODERN ART

Clare Oliver

Heinemann
LIBRARY

CONTENTS

WOODSTOCK
The hippie mantra of 'Turn On, Tune In, Drop Out' was experienced for one wild weekend in '69 at Woodstock, USA where the biggest-ever music festival was held.

ART IN FASHION
The '60s were a time of amazing cross-fertilisation, thanks to the rapid growth in the media, especially TV. No longer restricted to the gallery, art hit the catwalk. These outfits show the dazzling influence of Op Art.

REVOLUTIONS IN ART

The 1960s and '70s were a time of great experimentation in all aspects of culture. It is impossible to pinpoint a single dominant art style – art was exploding into every direction.

The period began with artists shaking off the influence of the Abstract Expressionists who had dominated the '50s. The Pop artists moved away from the interior world of emotion with pictures and sculptures of the shiny new goods that suddenly, it seemed, everyone had enough money to buy. Later, the Superrealists continued Pop's ideas with paintings that looked like photos and sculptures that looked like real people.

Abstract art really came into its own during the '60s and '70s – from the tightly-controlled visual treats of Op Art, to the experiments in colour theory that continued with the Minimalists.

Conceptualism was the most avant-garde of all the art movements. In this field, artists were using language, their own bodies, performance or even the environment to create startling pieces that made the viewer see the world afresh.

WHAAM!,
Roy Lichtenstein, 1963
Pop artist Roy Lichtenstein (1923–97) borrowed from everyday culture with his huge comic strip canvases.

POP MEETS ART
Central to youth culture was an explosion of popular music, with the Beatles breaking the hearts of millions of screaming fans. The cover for Sgt. Peppers *(above) was the work of British Pop artist Peter Blake (b. 1932) and his wife.*

MOVE IT!

At the beginning of the 20th century, the Constructivists in Russia had added a fourth dimension – movement – to sculpture, by incorporating machinery in their work. Moving sculpture popped up next in the USA in the 1930s, when Alexander Calder (1898–1976) began to make wind-powered mobiles.

THE POWER TO MOVE

Calder was the pioneer of Kinetic Art, or moving sculpture (from the Greek word *kinesis*). Some of his early pieces were motor-driven, but generally he relied on wind power. This introduced an element of chance – the movement of the mobile was random and unpredictable. Swiss artist Jean Tinguely (1925–91) used scrapped old machinery to power his sculptures. Often, they were designed to self-destruct.

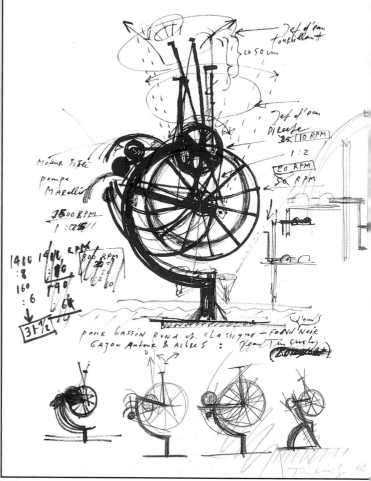

Au Bassin Rond et Classique, *Jean Tinguely, 1969*

FROM SKETCH TO SCULPTURE
Tinguely collected the elements for his sculpture from the local rubbish dump. Then he would draw plans of how they would fit together to make a moving sculpture, before making the piece for real.

ICE SCULPTURES

Why go to all the trouble of making art that won't last – or will even deliberately destroy itself? For many people, transcience (being short-lived) makes the experience of the art more beautiful, because the event is unique and cannot be repeated. This is part of the attraction of ice sculptures. In Ottawa, Canada, there is a display of ice sculptures for the Winterlude Festival each February. Each one may take more than a week of full-time work to sculpt.

Huge ice sculptures involve a lot of work, but are short-lived. They soon melt in the winter sunshine.

MODELS FOR RED, BLUE, AND BLACK
ALEXANDER CALDER, 1967

In this photo, Calder is in his studio with models for the huge, 14-metre-wide motorised mobile called *Red, Blue, and Black*. Calder once said that he wished to make 'moving Mondrians' – this can be seen in his choice of black, white and primary colours, and in his use of abstract shapes. *Red, Blue, and Black* was installed in Dallas Airport. Kinetic sculpture was a popular choice for public spaces. Its movement amused people while they were waiting or killing time.

HOMAGE TO NEW YORK

One of Tinguely's most famous pieces was *Homage to New York*. The artist assembled pieces of junk in front of the Museum of Modern Art in New York. The sculpture had all sorts of strange parts – pieces of piano, bicycle wheels and horns, a weather balloon and vials of smoke – and was designed to self-destruct. *Homage* did not work as planned. It burst into flames and New York's fire brigade had to be called! However, Tinguely was delighted with its ramshackle, spluttering performance. He wanted to make fun of people's blind faith in technology. Showing how quickly objects became silly and useless was his way of doing this.

MOVERS & BREAKERS

The name Auto-destructive Art came from its German-born pioneer, Gustav Metzger (*b.* 1926). For one of his pieces, performed in London in '61, Metzger spray-painted acid on to nylon. The acid burnt beautiful patterns into the fabric, but also destroyed the whole piece! Metzger did not like the way the art market reduced art to being about money. A piece that self-destructed provided the viewer with an experience, but could not be sold – it managed to escape the workings of the art market.

OP ART

Some art creates the illusion of movement, even though it does not actually move. This is known as Op Art, short for Optical Art. The term was coined by *Time Magazine* in 1964 and the following year the first Op Art exhibition was held at the Museum of Modern Art in New York.

POWERS OF PERCEPTION

This momentous exhibition, called 'The Responsive Eye', featured works by British artist Bridget Riley (*b.* 1931). Until about '66, Riley worked in a restricted palette of black and white. Pieces such as *Blaze I* ('62), *Fall* ('63) and *Descending* ('65) seem to spin, vibrate or move. When Riley introduced colour, it was as candy-coloured stripes – carefully chosen bold, bright hues that made each stripe seem to swizzle and rotate.

RILEY IN HER STUDIO
Riley said that an artist should be 'workman-like' in his or her approach. She uses studio assistants, not to create an emotional distance between herself and the art, but because it is practical.

COLOUR THEORY

Whether in monochrome or colour, Op was a type of abstraction. Richard Anuszkiewicz (*b.* 1930) was the leading Op artist in the USA. He had studied under Josef Albers (1888–1976), whose series of paintings called *Homage to the Square* (1949–76) explored the effects of different colour combinations. Albers placed smaller squares inside larger ones – depending on the colours used, these might seem to recede, advance or switch between the two. Anuszkiewicz continued his teacher's work, using coloured lines that radiated outwards.

IN BLACK AND WHITE
Op Art's geometric style captured the spirit of the time. Suddenly, optical patterns were everywhere! In '65 Riley had to sue a clothing firm in the USA for stealing her designs, and at the '68 Olympics, Op Art's influence could be seen in everything from the logo to the pavilions.

8

2170VP/106
VICTOR VASARELY, 1969

Hungarian-French artist Victor Vasarely (1908–97) was the father of Op Art. During the '30s Vasarely had worked as a poster designer in Paris. From the late '40s his paintings featured the same visual tricks that he had used in his advertising work. Most of his pieces aimed to achieve a three-dimensional effect through geometrical abstraction.

This piece shows how Vasarely applied simple rules to make the image project or recede. For instance, objects that are farther away look smaller. Vasarely used this rule to create the projecting globe at the top of the canvas. By making the spot pattern on the circle get smaller around the edges and also appear to bend, Vasarely turns it from a two-dimensional circle to a three-dimensional sphere. On the bottom half of this canvas, he does the opposite, creating an illusion of a hollow or indent by mapping the pattern so that it distorts and shrinks in towards the centre.

Vasarely thought that the artist was just an artisan, practising a trade or skill. Perhaps that's why he gave this piece a serial number, rather than a title.

OP ART BUILDING
During the '60s Vasarely lived and worked in the South of France. He believed that artists should be prolific, producing lots of work so that there was enough to go round and it would be available to ordinary people, not just an art world élite. He set up the Vasarely Foundation to display his work to the public and designed the building himself. The structure is a series of cubes and, with their alternate black-and-white circles, they are a giant embodiment of Op Art.

The Vasarely Foundation at Aix-en-Provence, France.

POP ART IN THE USA

Ask anyone to name an art movement of the 1960s and they'll probably come up with Pop Art. It had instant appeal. In the USA it was a reaction against the highly-charged (but exhausting) raw emotion favoured by the Abstract Expressionists.

FROM INSIDE TO OUT

Jackson Pollock (1912–56), the best-known Abstract Expressionist, had painted to express his deepest feelings. The backlash began when fellow-American Jasper Johns (*b.* 1930) started to experiment with everyday items, letting the method of copying them become art.

President Kennedy and wife Jackie on the day of his assassination in '63.

TRAGIC ICONS

The glamorous icons that Warhol chose to depict embodied the tragic side of fame. One of his subjects was Marilyn Monroe, the insecure sex symbol who died of an overdose in '62. Another was First Lady Jackie Kennedy, whose husband was shot dead in Dallas on November 22 the following year.

COOL STUFF

In the USA, the key Pop figures were Roy Lichtenstein, Andy Warhol (1928–87) and Swedish-born sculptor Claes Oldenburg (*b.* 1929). Warhol said Pop was about creating 'images that anyone could recognise in a split second…all the great modern things that the Abstract Expressionists had tried not to notice.' This meant comics, dollar bills, movie stars, junk foods, refrigerators and packaging – all the stuff of consumer culture. Oldenburg even called his studio 'The Store', filling it with plaster models of food or 'soft sculptures'.

POP ART TO SIT IN Jonathan Da Pas' 'Joe' chair ('70) paid tribute to popular baseball star Joe Di Maggio. It was inspired by the 'soft sculptures' made by Oldenburg – giant, squishy models of familiar objects such as burgers or lollipops.

10

LAUGHTER LINES

The choice of shallow, crude subject matter shifted the viewer's attention to the surface of the art and to the artist's methods. Pop images were taken out of their usual context, perhaps through enlargement, as in Lichtenstein's comic strips, or by the use of heightened, acid colours, as in Warhol's work. This forced the viewer to concentrate on form and composition, leaving the objects themselves behind. Lichtenstein said about his comic strips that 'Half the time they are upside down anyway when I work.'

WARHOL AND AN ASSISTANT
Assistants made Warhol's prints in his studio, called The Factory, but he often added extra colour with a brush.

COMIC EFFECT
Many of Lichtenstein's works, such as Whaam! ('63), were blown up from romance or war comics. Lichtenstein supplied just one or two frames of the story, so the images were out of context. The real subject matter was the way the art was made – the flat colour, thick black outlines and the precise representation of coloured dots, as on a print.

BRIT POP

The British brand of Pop Art was born in the 1950s when Richard Hamilton (*b.* 1922) created his Pop collage *Just What Is It That Makes Today's Homes So Different, So Appealing?* ('56) as a celebration and critique of glossy American consumerism.

GRADUATION DAY

Pop Art exploded with the 'Young Contemporaries' exhibition ('61). The artists were recent graduates of the Royal College of Art – David Hockney (*b.* 1937), R.B. Kitaj (*b.* 1932), Allen Jones (*b.* 1937) and Derek Boshier (*b.* 1937). Like Warhol, Hockney had a shock of dyed blonde hair, and a big personality. He was an instant celebrity and became a major success.

Ossie Clark at work in '69.

FASHION GURU

One of Hockney's most famous portraits was *Mr and Mrs Clark and Percy* ('70–71). It showed top fashion designer Ossie Clark (1942–96), his wife and pet cat. As in many of Hockney's pictures of friends, simple details suggested a modern and affluent lifestyle.

12

MOD STYLE
Baby-boomers born after World War II swelled a huge new youth market. Eager consumers of fashion, art and pop, they created their own unique styles.

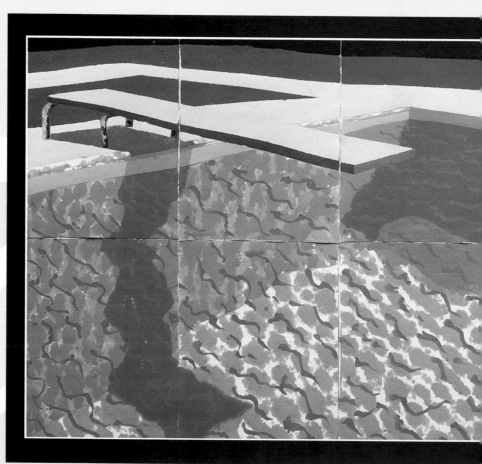

WHAT IS POP?

Richard Hamilton had famously listed the qualities of Pop in '57 – it was to be 'popular, transient, expendable, low-cost, mass-produced, young, witty, sexy, gimmicky, glamorous, and Big Business.' Brit Pop had an extra element – romance. Hockney's work often featured his lovers or Los Angeles, the love of his life.

POP FROM THE PAST

Pop artist Peter Blake (*b.* 1932) brought in romance through nostalgia, as seen in his design for the Beatles' album, *Sgt. Pepper's*. Usually working in collage, Blake depicted the pin-ups of the past, such as fairground strippers, wrestlers and boxers, as well as the pop and movie stars of the day. It was the Swinging Sixties. Britain was at the forefront of a cultural revolution in the fields of pop, film, photography and fashion as well as art.

SGT. PEPPER'S LONELY HEARTS CLUB BAND,
Peter Blake & Jann Haworth, 1967

COVER COLLAGE
Blake added popular artefacts such as toys, magazine cuttings and cinema tickets to his paintings. He first painted the Beatles in '62 and designed their '67 album with his wife.

13

THE DIVER
DAVID HOCKNEY, 1971

In '63 Hockney went to stay in Los Angeles, attracted by its easy living. His paintings of the city celebrate hot sunshine, blue pools, tall palms and modern buildings. Hockney's style was simple, but his desire to represent shadows, ripples or splashes graphically led him to try out different media – for this diptych, he used pressed paper pulp.

Hockney (right) moved to L.A. for good in '76.

SIGNIFICANT ART

When Marcel Duchamp (1887–1969) had displayed his 'ready-made' urinal and presented it as art – *Fountain* ('17) – Conceptualism was born. From that moment, the idea or concept behind the art could be more important than the actual piece.

THE IDEA OF ART

In '67 American artist Sol LeWitt (*b.* 1928) wrote, 'In Conceptual Art the idea or concept is the most important aspect…The idea becomes the machine that makes

SIGNS & LOGOS
This is the logo for the famous fashion store, Biba, in London. In posters and ads, words and images fuse to create a new meaning that signifies the brand.

the art.' One of the recurring ideas behind Conceptual Art is how to convey meaning. Many artists of the '60s and '70s used words to do this – for example the Americans Robert Rauschenberg (*b.* 1925), Robert Barry (*b.* 1936) and Joseph Kosuth (*b.* 1945) and the loose, English collective of artists known as Art & Language, founded in the late '60s.

DEFINING ART

Kosuth went further than most in using language as the material and also the subject of his art. Many of his works featured magnified dictionary definitions. His piece *One and Three Chairs* ('65) displayed a real chair, a same-size photograph of it and the definition for the word 'chair'. Kosuth disconcerts the viewer by presenting different realities, questioning the way we define things – which best represents a chair?

LANGUAGE AND STRUCTURALISM

Joseph Kosuth's initial interest in dictionary definitions soon expanded to take in the meanings in literature and academic texts. This was a particular preoccupation of the '60s and '70s, following the appearance of a movement known as Structuralism in France. The Structuralists were concerned with meaning. Although mostly focussing on literature, they wanted to know and show how anything – from a bus ticket to a novel, an advertisement to a work of art – puts across its meaning. They tried to identify a set of rules that would explain methods of communication. They based their work on the studies of signs and symbols made by the Swiss scholar, Ferdinand de Saussure (1857–1913). French Structuralist Roland Barthes (1915–80) believed that a novel or a work of art was simply a system of signs and that the viewer actively created the meaning for themselves. This annoyed some people, because it meant the author or artist was no longer responsible for creating the meaning.

MIND OVER MATTER
If a urinal could be art because the artist said so, then so could anything! Rauschenberg's piece for a Parisian exhibition in '60 was a telegram with these words (left)

THIS IS A PORTRAIT OF IRIS CLERT IF I SAY SO

14

ALL KINDS OF MEANING

Dictionary definitions aim to be as precise as possible. In the same way, an artist might try to distil an idea so that its meaning is clear to the viewer. But many of the language pieces prove how impossible this is. Words are ambiguous, the viewer's response unpredictable. For example, in *It is…Inconsistent* ('71), Robert Barry projected 21 slides with short descriptive phrases such as 'It is purposeful', or 'It is influenced.' Did these describe art in general or the particular piece (Barry's choice of adjectives, the order in which he showed the slides, and so on)? Perhaps, but the viewer could just as easily choose to relate them to more personal matters, such as their own emotions or relationships. All of this self-referential art recognised that the artist's point of view was not important, because the viewers actively create their own meanings anyway.

Roland Barthes was a key Structuralist.

INVESTIGATION 8, PROPOSITION 2
JOSEPH KOSUTH, 1970

Kosuth believed that avoiding traditional art forms 'provided the possibility of seeing how art acquires meaning.' In this installation, each clock is set differently, challenging ideas of recording time. As in many of his *Investigations*, the exercise books contain theoretical writings. Kosuth often quoted from the philosopher Wittgenstein (1889–1951) who in '21 had argued that every sentence is a picture of the fact that it represents, although he later rejected this.

INVISIBLE ART

Conceptualism had prioritised the *idea* of art rather than the physical artwork – a logical next step was to do away with the art object altogether. For some critics, invisible art was a case of 'The Emperor's New Clothes.' But was it really a con? New York artist Robert Barry once said that 'Nothing seems to me the most potent thing in the world.' What's more, invisible art could be an effective way to suggest that there is no meaning to life.

SOLDIERS IN VIETNAM
For Placid Civil Monument *(1967), America artist Claes Oldenburg employed a team of grave-diggers to dig and then refill a grave. This invisible art was a protest about the Vietnam War (1955–75). It implied that the sacrifice of soldiers in the war would also ultimately disappear without trace.*

16

MERDA D'ARTISTA
PIERO MANZONI, 1961

The Italian artist Piero Manzoni (1933–63) was one of the first to play with invisible art. In '59 he started drawing lines on sheets of paper which he rolled up and sealed in boxes. On each box he put the line's length, when it was drawn and his signature. Of course, the buyer or viewer could not open the box to check there really was a line inside – if they did, they would destroy the art! The same was true of Manzoni's limited edition of 90 *Merda d'Artista* – tins of his own excrement. But the important thing is the *idea* that the tin contains his excrement and what it says about the act of creating (and selling) art. Sadly Manzoni's career was cut short. He died of liver failure at 30, after years of excess drinking.

THROWING IT ALL AWAY

French artist Yves Klein (1928–62) was obsessed by emptiness, which he called *Le Vide* (the void). In '59 he began selling 'Zones of Immaterial Pictorial Sensibility' (in other words, non-existent art). Buyers were given a *Receipt for the Immaterial*, which they had to burn, destroying any evidence that they 'owned' the 'art'. They had paid Klein in gold leaf – in '62, he scattered half of this into the waters of the River Seine, recording the ritual in photographs. So this 'immaterial', non-art materialised itself – not only in all the ideas, effort and rituals involved in carrying out the project, but also by surviving in photos.

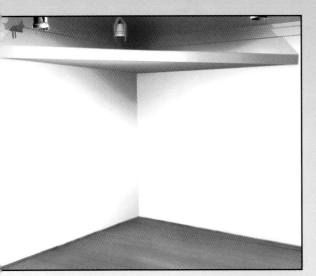

*ARTIST IN RESIDENCE
For his exhibition 'White Light/White Heat' ('74), American artist Chris Burden (b. 1946) lay on a high shelf, hidden from view. The gallery itself was empty! Part of the art experience was deciding if you really believed that the artist was there.*

DOCUMENTING THE INVISIBLE

This creates an interesting dilemma. Is the art truly invisible if there is a photo that records the event, or even a written description of it? The American Robert Barry was one of the most extreme of the Conceptualists. He was famous for taking photos of transparent gases being released into the air, or of transparent threads strung between trees – none of which could be seen. The 'invisible' art remained invisible, even to the camera!

NOTHING MATTERS

Barry's weirdest work was *Telepathic Piece* ('69). He wrote in the exhibition catalogue 'During the exhibition, I will try to communicate telepathically a work of art, the nature of which is a series of thoughts that are not applicable to language or image.'

17

HOT AIR?

In '19 Marcel Duchamp displayed his *L'Air de Paris*. This was a ready-made glass ampoule that Duchamp had broken open and then resealed. It is a beautiful object in its own right, but the idea is supreme. Piero Manzoni, too, sold air. His boxes of 'artist's breath' contained a balloon with a display stand, which could be purchased as they were, or inflated by the artist – eventually they would deflate anyway.

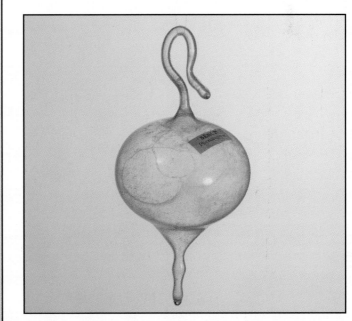

L'AIR DE PARIS, *Marcel Duchamp, 1919*

ART'S HAPPENING

Questions that the Conceptual artists were asking included 'What is art?' or 'What form should art take?' During the 1960s and '70s, the distinction between art and theatre blurred. Performance as art sprang up everywhere, in hippie happenings and at festivals all over the world.

STRADIVARIUS VIOLIN Typically, Performance Ar was chaotic or absurd In '62, Nam June Pai performed his One fo Violin Solo, where h smashed a violin to pieces. He reckoned tha the better the quality o the violin, the better th sound of its destruction

THE WEIRD WORLD OF FLUXUS

Originating in Germany, Fluxus was an international art movement of the early '60s that revived the mad, disruptive spirit of Dada. Fluxus Festivals were held across Europe and also in New York, with strange performances by artists, musicians and dancers. Fluxus artists included the Germans Joseph Beuys (1921–86) and Wolf Vostell (*b.* 1932), the Frenchman Robert Filliou (1926–87) and the Americans George Maciunas (1931–78), Dick Higgins (*b.* 1938), Nam June Paik (*b.* 1932) and Yoko Ono (*b.* 1933). One of Beuys' most famous performances was *How to Explain Pictures to a Dead Hare* ('65), when he smeared his face with honey and gold leaf, then walked around holding a dead hare, talking about pictures to it.

JOHN & YOKO Japanese-born American Yoko Ono was a well known performance artist in her own right before marriage to the Beatle John Lennon brought her international fame. For their honeymoon in March '69 (right) they staged a 'love-in' – a kind of happening at which they made a plea for peace.

HAIR PEACE.

BED PEACE.

THE SINGING SCULPTURE

GILBERT & GEORGE, 1970

When Italian-born Gilbert Proesch (*b.* 1943) and Brit George Passmore (*b.* 1942) first met in '67, they decided to make their whole lives one long piece of art. They became Gilbert & George and have lived and worked together ever since. Their earl pieces were 'living sculptures' – for *The Singing Sculpture,* they stood on a table and duetted the song *Underneath the Arches* for eight hours! After '77 their work moved to what they call photo-pieces, giant panels of brightly-tinted black-and-white prints of themselves.

18

STUDENT UPRISINGS

During the '60s there was an optimistic belief in the power of demonstrations. The protest in Paris in '68 (which Wolf Vostell called 'the greatest Happening of all') escalated into a national crisis and led to an overhaul of French education. And in '69 Germany's Dusseldorf Academy briefly closed after a rebellion led by artist and professor Joseph Beuys.

Riot police (right) on the streets of Paris in May '68.

ANTI-ART

Fluxus published many manifestos outlining its aims. It wanted to release people from their inhibitions and to 'purge the world of dead art...to promote living art, anti-art.' This goal was shared by other performance artists. In order to free people to experience art more fully, many were deliberately provocative, to shake up cosy traditions.

ART WITH A MESSAGE

Beuys said that politics was 'social sculpture'. Like many of the artists, he had a political agenda. Common issues included anti-capitalism, equality for women or more sexual freedom. In their work, Gilbert & George confront preconceptions about homosexuality by openly presenting themselves as a gay couple. They point out 'Our reason for making pictures is to change people and not to congratulate them on being how they are.'

LAND ART

The hippies' back-to-nature ideals were about escaping the artificiality of the urban environment. In the same spirit, a new type of sculpture emerged, as artists returned to the natural landscape and began making their own, modern-day earthworks.

Zen rock garden, Japan

SPIRITUALITY IN THE GARDEN
Monks in Japan have raised the garden to an art form, creating 'dry landscapes' as places for calm and peace. Zen gardens feature groups of rocks, with each one carefully positioned in a sea of gravel. The gravel is raked daily to create fluid ripples. The act of raking is a form of meditation, which can lead to enlightenment – the state of supreme understanding that all Buddhists strive to reach.

ROLLING STONES

Land artists include Robert Smithson (1938–73) and James Turrell (*b.* 1941) in the USA, and Richard Long (*b.* 1945) and Andy Goldsworthy (*b.* 1956) in Britain. Smithson's *Spiral Jetty* ('70) was a spiral of rocks projecting into Great Salt Lake, Utah. Like much Land Art its shape was organic and the piece was temporary, because after a few years the lake's level rose and drowned it. Some of Long's pieces were simply lines of flattened grass where he had walked.

IT'S A WRAP!

Bulgarian-born Christo (*b.* 1935) and his French wife Jeanne-Claude (*b.* 1935) create unique environmental works. Some of it, called *empaquetage*, involves wrapping things up. They raise the money for each project by selling plans and drawings and will not accept grants or donations, in case it compromises their art. They want to keep their art pure.

Stonehenge exudes mystery – and spirituality. Prehistoric stone circles are an inspiration to Land artists.

RUNNING FENCE
CHRISTO AND
JEANNE-CLAUDE, 1976

Christo and Jeanne-Claude create new environments by introducing new elements. They believe this helps people to view things with new eyes. They like to work in fabric, Christo explains, because it allows people to see 'things that cannot usually be seen, like the wind blowing, or the Sun reflecting in ways it had not before.' For two weeks in September '76, their 5.5-metre-high curtain of white nylon stretched for almost 40 kilometres across California, down to the Pacific. It took the couple three-and-a-half years of plans and meetings, and 18 public hearings, to bring their mega project off. In urban environments they have wrapped whole buildings including the Pont Neuf, Paris ('75–'85).

One of the Christos' most ambitious projects was Surrounded Islands ('83), off the Florida coast which, again, lasted just 14 days. They surrounded 11 islands with floating rafts of fuchsia-pink fabric. Seen from the air, they looked like ballerinas' tutus. Unfurling more than 600,000 square metres of fabric took a lot of organisation. Christo (right) zoomed around in a speedboat shouting directions.

LESS IS MORE

To its critics, Minimalist Art seems to show nothing much at all. This art movement rose up in the 1950s and has flourished to the present day. Its subject matter is completely pared down, so the viewer is free from any distraction. Minimalism focuses on space, form and physical presence. Like Land Art, it allows the viewer to view the world with fresh eyes, and explore what beauty – and art – is all about.

The sleeve for the Beatles' White album ('68) was pure white. In contrast to the crammed, busy record sleeves of the day, it appeared simple, crisp and clean.

SCULPTURAL EXPERIENCE

The three key Minimalist sculptors are the Americans Donald Judd (1928–94), Dan Flavin (1933–96) and Carl Andre (b. 1935). All three have specialised in one particular shape or form, repeatedly using it in different works. Judd, for example, is known for his wall-mounted 'ladders' of boxes. A typical work by Flavin would be a bare neon tube at an angle. Andre's 'floor pieces' are arrangements of identical or contrasting tiles or blocks.

Atheneum Visitor Center, designed by Richard Meier.

LAWS OF ORDER
For his Atheneum Visitor Center ('79) in Indiana, USA, architect Richard Meier (b. 1934) made clever use of pure white walls. Their simple curves and lines allowed him to bring 'interior' elements, such as stairs and walkways, outside and make a feature of their form, without making the whole appear too cluttered.

EQUIVALENT VIII
CARL ANDRE, 1966

Though Andre's eight *Equivalent* sculptures are made of building bricks, the inspiration came from nature, while Andre was canoeing. He has arranged them to be low and horizontal, like water on a lake. It can be hard to see what makes a pile of bricks art, and when the Tate bought this piece in '76, there was an outcry. Andre wanted to alter the viewer's sense of space. Some of his other pieces are even designed to be walked on, to really change the way the viewer relates to the gallery space that a piece is in.

American sculptor Carl Andre (right).

MONOCHROME MAGIC

Minimalism also appealed to painters, such as the Americans Frank Stella (b. 1936), Ad Reinhardt (1913–67) and Robert Ryman (b. 1930). From the late '50s until his death, Reinhardt did a series of all-black paintings which had faint patterns in different shades of black.

These influenced Ryman, who paints only white squares. Despite (or rather, because of) these restrictions, Ryman has been hugely adventurous. He has experimented with white oil paint, acrylic, emulsion, enamel and pastels. As well as traditional canvas, he has made works on wood, plexiglass and steel. He is super-sensitive to how the smallest nuance, such as the thickness of a brushstroke, can transform the painting.

23

REALLY REAL

In the late 1960s, a new style of art appeared in the USA, partly born out of Pop and the reaction against Abstract Expressionism. Variously called Super, Photo, New or Hyper Realism, it presented ordinary people with warts-and-all reality.

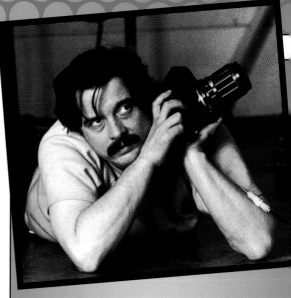

Fashion photographer David Bailey hard at work with his trusty camera.

CLOSE-UP CANVASES

American artist Chuck Close (*b*. 1940), the greatest of the Superrealist painters, always fought against being pigeonholed. In '97 he explained 'I stayed out of all those Realist shows. I refused to participate not because I hated all that work but because I just wanted to be seen as an individual.' Close's first colossal painting from a passport-style photo was *Self-Portrait* ('68) – he is still making his 'heads' today. His method is to pencil a grid on to a Polaroid snap of the subject, then transfer the image, square by square, to a giant canvas.

CAUGHT ON CAMERA

British photographer David Bailey (*b*. 1938) exploded on to the '60s fashion scene. His relaxed snapping style produced realistic, natural-looking studies of his models. He captured all the popular icons of the decade – actors Michael Caine and Catherine Deneuve, model Jean Shrimpton and a whole host of pop stars, including Marianne Faithful and Mick Jagger. Bailey was so influential that he became an icon himself, and he inspired the director Michelangelo Antonioni to make the thriller *Blow-Up* ('66) about a cool young photographer in Swinging London.

HORRIBLE HANSON

The major Superrealist sculptor was American Duane Hanson (1925–96), who made sculptures of ordinary, everyday people in polyester resin or fibreglass. His approach is *so* realistic that the images are highly unflattering. Hanson explained 'To me, the resignation, emptiness and loneliness of their existence captures the true reality of life for these people.'

Hanson dressed his figures in real clothes, and gave them real 'accessories', such as pebble-lensed glasses and shopping bags. The characters always seem to be struggling.

YOUNG WOMAN SHOPPER, *Duane Hanson, 1973*

24

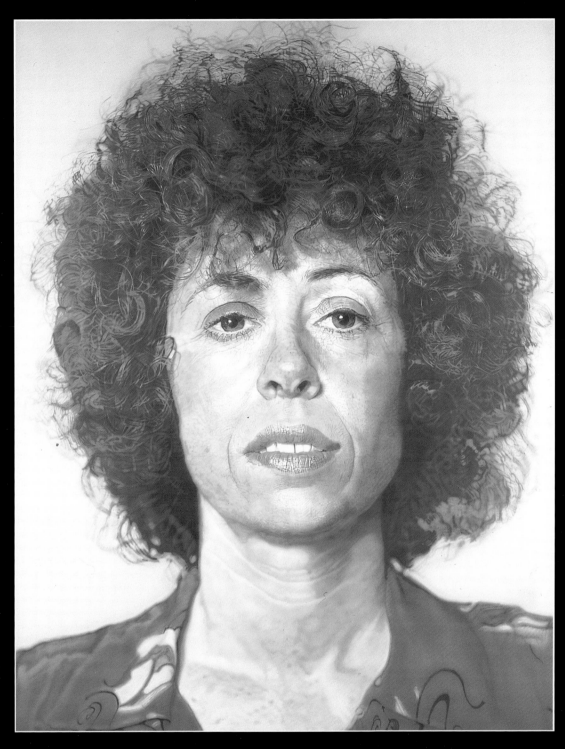

LINDA
CHUCK CLOSE, 1975–6

Close's works are all titled by the first names of the sitters, and they all dwarf the viewer – this canvas is 2.74 metres high! Not all are paintings – he also used thumb-prints and collages of paper pulp, for example. But whatever the method, from a distance they look just like photographs.

Faithful to the original photo, Close paints only some parts in focus. Linda's face is so sharp that the viewer can see the creases on her skin and even her veins, but at the edges, her hair appears fuzzy. Close said that he wanted to make his works 'impersonal and personal, arm's-length and intimate.'

DOWN UNDER

The Aboriginals of Australia have been making art for perhaps 40,000 years. Their art is sacred, depicting the myths and beliefs that connect them to the land and to their ancestors.

After white colonisation in the 19th century, Aboriginals were forced off their ancestral land. Their art came to show a dialogue between the old myths and their feelings of separation from them.

26

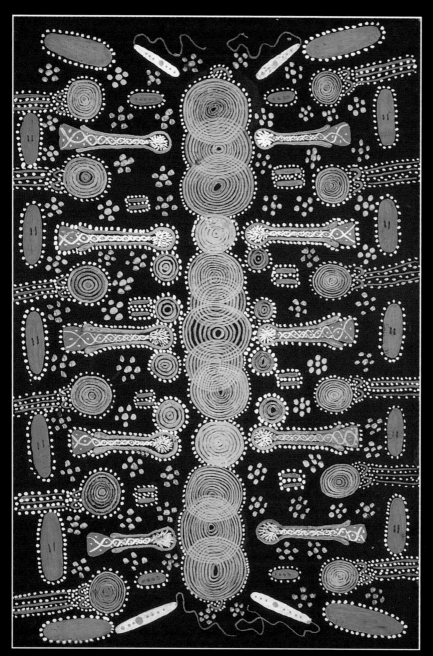

MEN'S DREAMING
TIM LEURA TJAPALTJARRI, 1971

Tim Leura Tjapaltjarri (1939–84) and his brother Clifford Possum Tjapaltjarri (*b.c.* 1932) were two of the first Aboriginal artists to experiment with traditional-style paintings for the international art market. In the '70s they moved to Panunya and became part of the Panunya Tula Artists. The brothers collaborated on *Warlugulong* ('76), the finest Aboriginal work of the '70s. Tjapaltjarri often painted the Dreaming. Each line, circle and dot has several different levels of meaning – understanding them all requires deep knowledge of Aboriginal myth. Artists never revealed the meaning, but non-Aboriginals appreciate the style anyway, for its beautiful geometric abstraction.

Body-painting (right), too, uses earthy colours and sacred motifs.

OCHRE TO ACRYLIC, BARK TO BOARD

Traditionally, Aboriginal art was painted on rocks and eucalyptus bark, using natural pigments. In the early '70s, Geoffrey Bardon, a schoolteacher at the Panunya settlement, changed all that. Bardon wanted the children to learn about the art of their own culture, so he asked elders from Panunya to paint on the school walls. When their mural *Honey Ant Dreaming* ('71) was finished, the elders went on, painting on boards, old doors and even lino using pigments mixed with acrylics or PVA. They put 620 pieces on sale, to raise money for more materials, including canvases. Before long, their work had a huge international following.

FREEDOM FIGHTERS
Since the '60s, Aboriginals have fought hard for equal rights. They were not included on Australia's national census until '67, which meant they were not considered full citizens. In '76, the Aboriginal Land Rights Act restored some of their land.

SACRED MOUNTAIN

Uluru (also known as Ayer's Rock) is a massive outcrop of rock in Western Australia. It held special significance in the myths of the Aboriginals, but it was not returned to them until '85. Uluru changes through the day, over a rich spectrum of reds and browns. Aboriginals employ these colours in their art and often use ochre, a natural pigment from the iron-rich earth.

Uluru is enormous, rising 348 metres high and stretching for 3.6 kilometres.

MAPPING MYTH

The Dreaming was the beginning of Aboriginal culture. Traditional stories tell of the Ancestors, magical half-human beings, who walked the land and made it good for humans. These stories can be told as pictures, and some Aboriginal art is best seen as a map. The artists work with their pieces flat on the ground, and the art can be viewed from any angle.

MORINGEA OUTSTATION
Many Aboriginals were forced into government settlements, but some moved to outstations, small communities on their own land, like this one in the Northern Territory, photographed in '78.

LATIN AMERICAN ART

In the 1960s and '70s South American artists were working in wide-ranging styles. No single movement dominated as Muralism had during the '20s and '30s. Many artists left their countries of birth and went to Europe and the USA, either to study there for a few years, or to settle there for good.

INTERNATIONAL STYLE

Venezuelans Jésus Rafael Soto (*b.* 1923) and Carlos Cruz-Diez (*b.* 1923), based in Paris, made Kinetic Art. Soto is famous for his 'vibration sculptures' – constructions of hanging wires designed to be moved by the viewer.

THE BRILLIANCE OF BOTERO

The most famous of the 'ex-pats' is Colombian artist Fernando Botero (*b.* 1932), who has lived in New York and Paris. Botero's paintings are very distinctive – and people either love them or loathe them. They all feature strange characters that might have been blown up with a bicycle pump! Botero's painting style is rich and lavish and his work fetches high prices.

28

Kennedy meets his commanders.

FOLK ART
This cheery papier-mache sculpture is typical of those made to celebrate the Day of the Dead (November 2nd). The skeletons decorate the tombs of dead relatives.

AFTER VELAZQUEZ: MARGUERITA
FERNANDO BOTERO, 1977

Botero started to paint his 'fat' figures in the early '60s. Many are reworkings of famous paintings by Caravaggio (1571–1610), Velázquez (1599–1660) or Goya (1746–1828). These belong to the ages of the Spanish *conquistadores* and the colonial powers that succeeded them. Many of Botero's contemporaries rejected all things Spanish on political grounds, but not him. Instead, he reclaims and transforms the richness of his Spanish heritage, making it his own. 'Whether they appear fat or not does not interest me,' he said. 'It has hardly any meaning for my painting. My concern is with formal fullness, abundance.'

MEXICO AFTER MURALISM

In Mexico, art was struggling to be truly 'Mexican' without repeating the heroic, Aztec-style murals of Diego Rivera (1886–1957). Many artists looked to Rufino Tamayo (1899–1991), a contemporary of Rivera's who drew heavily from folk art and whose parents had been Zapotec Indians. Tamayo used deep, sumptuous colours, in thick layers of paint. He continued to produce powerful pieces late in life – *Mascara Rojo* ('77) depicts a tortured figure that calls to mind a Day of the Dead skeleton. Tamayo was the major influence on Francisco Toledo (*b.* 1940). Toledo's *The Lazy Dog* ('72) makes a feature of its primitive outlines and thick texture.

*ROYAL FAVOURITE
Velázquez was just 24
when Philip IV of Spain
made him court painter.
Las Meninas (The Maids
of Honour) was one of the
artist's last paintings. It
shows Philip's daughter,
Princess Marguerita. The
loving detail with which
Velázquez rendered fabrics
was a big influence on Botero.*

LAS MENINAS,
Diego Velázquez, 1656

GLOSSARY

ABSTRACTION Expressing meaning through shapes and colours, rather than realism.

ABSTRACT EXPRESSIONISM Art style born in the '40s to express emotion through paint and painting techniques.

AUTO-DESTRUCTIVE ART Art that destroys itself.

AVANT-GARDE Pioneering or experimental.

COMPOSITION The way the elements of a work of art make a satisfactory whole.

CONCEPTUAL ART Art where the idea is paramount, such as Minimalism or Land Art.

CONSTRUCTIVISM Abstract art movement that developed in Russia pre-'17, and used industrial materials.

DADA An anti-sense and anti-tradition movement in art and literature born in World War I.

DIPTYCH Artwork that is presented on a pair of panels.

FORM The individual shapes in a work of art, and the relationships between them.

HAPPENING An event.

KINETIC ART Sculpture that incorporates movement.

LAND ART Art that uses natural materials and may be part of the landscape.

MINIMALISM An abstract style of art which uses very simple forms or limited colour.

MURALISM Mexican movement of mural painting from the '20s.

OP ART Art that creates an optical illusion.

PERFORMANCE ART Art based on theatre, dance, or some other type of performance.

POP ART Art style popular from the '50s–'70s that uses the imagery of popular culture.

READY-MADE A manufactured object chosen and presented by the artist as a work of art.

STRUCTURALISM Form of literary criticism that said readers actively create meaning.

SUPERREALISM Also known as Hyperrealism or Photo Realism. Art style that records every detail with photographic accuracy.

TELEPATHY Transmitting ideas through thought, without words.

30

WORLD EVENTS

- USSR: Leonid Brezhnev becomes president
- Yuri Gagarin in space
- Berlin Wall is built
- Cuban Missile Crisis
- Algerian independence
- USA: President Kennedy assassinated
- Vietnam War begins
- S. Africa: Mandela jailed
- UK: capital punishment abolished
- China: Cultural Revolution begins
- Six-Day War between Arabs & Israelis
- Paris: Student Riots
- Aswan Dam completed
- Neil Armstrong is the first man on the Moon
- PLO hijack four planes
- US troops to Cambodia
- Uganda: Amin seizes power
- Greenpeace founded
- Aboriginal Tent Embassy
- US troops leave Vietnam
- Chile: Pinochet in power
- Yom Kippur War; oil crisis
- USA: Watergate Scandal
- Turkey invades Cyprus
- Pol Pot's Khmer Rouge take over Cambodia
- Viking landers on Mars
- Aboriginal Land Rights Act
- UN sanctions arms sales to S. Africa
- Vatican: election of Pope John Paul II
- UK: Thatcher becomes PM
- Iran: Fall of the Shah

TIMELINE

ART	DESIGN	THEATRE & FILM	BOOKS & MUSIC
•Klein: IKB 79 •Tinguely: Homage to New York	•Brazil: Niemeyer & Costa's Plaza of the Three Powers	•Hitchcock's Psycho •Fellini's La Dolce Vita	•La Monte Young: Poem for Tables, Chairs, Benches
•Oldenburg: 'The Store' •Manzoni: Merda d'Artista	•Saarinen's TWA Terminal at Idlewild (now JFK) Airport	•Broadway: West Side Story •Peter Hall forms the RSC	•Joseph Heller: Catch 22 •Günter Grass: The Tin Drum
•Warhol: Marilyn Diptych	•Giacomo & Castiglioni: 'Arco' lamp	•David Lean's Lawrence of Arabia	•Burgess: A Clockwork Orange •Lessing: The Golden Notebook
•Lichtenstein: Whaam! •Soto: Horizontal Movement	•Gropius & Belluschi's Pan-Am Building, New York	•Peter Sellers stars as Dr. Strangelove	•Beach Boys: Surfin' USA
•Bridget Riley: Current •Warhol film: Empire State	•Japan: Kenzo Tange's Olympic Sports Halls	•Andrews as Mary Poppins •Harrison in My Fair Lady	•The Kinks: You Really Got Me
•Beuys: Explaining Paintings to a Dead Hare	•Aarnio: 'Globe' chair •YSL: 'Mondrian' dress	•P. Hall directs The Homecoming •Godard: Alphaville	•Sonny & Cher: I Got You, Babe •Sylvia Plath: Ariel
•Carl Andre: Lever	•F. Saroglia designs the wool trademark symbol	•Taylor & Burton in Who's Afraid of Virginia Woolf?	•Capote: In Cold Blood •Dylan: Blonde on Blonde
•Gilbert & George meet •Warhol: Marilyn	•Canada: Moshe Safdie's Habitat Housing	•Hippie musical Hair •Le Grand Meaulnes	•Warhol is producer on The Velvet Underground & Nico
•USA: 'Earthworks' exhibition	•USA: Lake Point Tower, a curved glass block of flats	•2001: A Space Odyssey •Planet of the Apes	•The Beatles: White Album •Hendrix: Electric Ladyland
•Kosuth writes 'Art after Philosophy' article	•Kawakubo founds Comme des Garçons	•Orton: What the Butler Saw •Fonda in Easy Rider	•Georges Perec: A Void •Woodstock Music Festival
•Hanson: Tourists •Smithson: Spiral Jetty	•P. Max's 'Love' poster •De Pas: 'Joe' chair	•Aboriginal culture hits the big screen with Walkabout	•Greer: The Female Eunuch •Jackson 5: ABC
•Richter: Brigitte Polk •Long: Connemara, Ireland	•Paris: Piano & Rogers' Pompidou Centre (to '77)	•Lloyd Webber & Rice's Jesus Christ Superstar	•The Doors: L.A. Woman •Updike: Rabbit Redux
•Ellsworth Kelly: Yellow Red Curve I	•Switzerland: Botta's Bianchi House	•Brando in The Godfather •Tarkovsky's Solaris	•Italo Calvino: Invisible Cities •Moog synthesizer patented
•Chuck Close: Leslie	•Utzon's Sydney Opera House finally completed	•Luis Buñuel: The Discreet Charm of the Bourgeoisie	•Thomas Pynchon: Gravity's Rainbow
•Botero: Alof de Wignacourt (after Caravaggio)	• Des-in studio: 'Tire' sofa	•Jack Nicholson stars in Chinatown	•ABBA: Waterloo •Barry Manilow: Mandy
•Burden: White Light/ White Heat •Cragg: Stack	•Britain: Lasdun's National Theatre	•Spielberg's Jaws •Monty Python & the Holy Grail	•Eno: Another Green World •Salman Rushdie: Grimus
•Christo & Jeanne-Claude: Running Fence	•Kenneth Grange styles high-speed 125 train	•Stallone: Rocky •Bowie in The Man Who Fell to Earth	•Philip Glass & Robert Wilson: Einstein on the Beach
•Rufino Tamayo: Mascara Rojo	•Milton Glaser's 'I ♥ NY' logo	•George Lucas: Star Wars •Saturday Night Fever	•Sex Pistols: God Save the Queen
•USA: 'Bad Painting' exhibition	•UK: Foster's Sainsbury Centre for Visual Arts, UEA	•Parker: Midnight Express •Pinter: Betrayal	•Hockney designs set for the opera The Magic Flute
•Judy Chicago: The Dinner Party	•Sony Walkman •Meier's Atheneum Visitor Center	•Ridley Scott: Alien •Coppola: Apocalypse Now	•Kundera: The Book of Laughter and Forgetting

INDEX